Original title:
The Sun's Embrace

Copyright © 2025 Creative Arts Management OÜ
All rights reserved.

Author: Clara Whitfield
ISBN HARDBACK: 978-1-80581-637-9
ISBN PAPERBACK: 978-1-80581-164-0
ISBN EBOOK: 978-1-80581-637-9

Sunbeams on Autumn Leaves

Golden rays play hide and seek,
While squirrels dance and birds all squeak.
A leaf pirouette in the air,
Shouts, 'Catch me if you dare!'

Pumpkins chuckle in the glow,
While acorns roll, putting on a show.
Nature laughs, oh what a scene,
In the warmth, all seems serene.

Glimmers of a New Dawn

Morning light with a wink so bright,
Takes off pajamas, ready for flight.
Roosters crow, and coffee brews,
While sleepyheads choose snooze or clues.

The world yawns, stretching its arms,
While trees giggle with leafy charms.
The cat does flips in the light's embrace,
Chasing shadows all over the place.

Daybreak's Gentle Kiss

Awake, awake! The sun's on stage,
A cheeky grin, the perfect mage.
It tickles the flowers with buttery rays,
Prompting them to dance in a sunny craze.

Bumblebees buzz their morning tune,
While the daisies play 'howdy' to the moon.
Oh look, the clouds are wearing socks,
As the sun rolls in like a friendly ox.

Warmth of the Sky's Heart

In a sky so blue, a warmth so sweet,
Birds wear sunglasses, dancing on their feet.
A picnic basket means ants parade,
With tiny marching bands unafraid.

Butterflies flutter, showing off their flair,
As children giggle and run without care.
Grasshoppers leap, playing hopscotch grand,
In this sunlit playground, life is unplanned.

Luminous Touch of the Morning

Bright beams burst through my window's glass,
I squint and swear, 'What a sunburned mass!'
A coffee cup swims in my sleepy hand,
While birds are chirping in their own band.

A sock monster dances in the twilight breeze,
Looking for its partner, oh such a tease!
I trip on my thoughts, just like on the floor,
This day's just begun, who could ask for more?

Embrace of the Golden Hour

As daylight shines with a silly grin,
The cat steals my chair, the furball wins!
I attempt to bask with sunshine's laugh,
But ants parade across my photograph.

Mindless of my plans, the grill grows hot,
While I chase my dreams—hey, where's that pot?
Friends gather round, and we all take seat,
With laughter that sizzles and summer heat.

Flickering Shadows Beneath Rays

Shadows prance in the garden's play,
Turns out my fence was a dance ballet!
Grasshoppers hum their own silly tune,
As I step on a rake—who knew it was June!

In shades of green, I start to complain,
Why do my legs feel so stiff and in pain?
The breeze tickles, and I shout, "No fair!"
While my sun hat flies like a kite in the air!

Sunshine's Tender Serenade

The field turns gold with giggles and glee,
I follow a butterfly—oh wait, that's me!
With lemonade dreams, we clink our cups,
And catch a case of the silly hiccups.

A picnic spread, oh what a spread,
But ants have their plans, no crumbs left for bread!
We dance in the glow, under clouds that roam,
This laughter-filled day feels just like home.

Harmony in Solar Skies

Beams of gold bounce off my head,
My hair's a bus-stop for rays instead.
Birds sing, squirrels start to dance,
I trip on grass; it's a bright romance.

Sunshine giggles with every glance,
While I try to enjoy this chance.
Wit and whimsy in every hue,
A tan line that says, 'I'm not so blue!'

Love Letters of Dappled Sunlight

Letters from light drop on my face,
A cheeky wink, a warm embrace.
"Dear human," they scribble in heat,
"Don't forget to dance on your feet!"

While grass stains laugh, I plop on the ground,
Messy and joyful, no sense to be found.
Sunbeams scatter, a playful tease,
Whispering secrets through rustling trees.

Tender Tendrils of Light

Tendrils of warmth stretch far and wide,
Playing tag with shadows that slide.
I'm caught in a sparkle, how silly is that?
As a butterfly lands on my oversized hat.

Chasing the beams like a child with glee,
Where's the prism? Come play hide and seek with me!
Giggling clouds join in the game,
While I bask in this golden fame.

Wrapped in Stardust and Light

Wrapped in rays like a burrito,
I squint at a bright and noisy amigo.
With every laugh, the shadows grow thin,
As dreams made of light start to spin.

Joking with photons, I start to believe,
That even the mundane can dance, and conceive.
A festival of colors bursts from above,
Where sunlight plays peek-a-boo with love.

Serenity Found in Solar Corners

In golden rays, the cats do bask,
With tiny hats, it's quite the task.
They squint and stretch, oh what a sight,
While plotting sneaky naps till night.

A bird joins in with chirps so clear,
He sings of cheese and sunny beer.
The flowers giggle, roots in play,
While ants in suits march on their way.

Their laughter drips like melting ice,
As shadows dance, oh how nice!
Among the blooms, they share a laugh,
The sunbeams serve the finest staff.

A dog rolls over, tongue out wide,
Thinking the garden is his slide.
With a woof, he claims the space,
He dreams of chasing rays with grace.

Embered Dreams of Luminescent Light

The kitchen's warm with toasty cheer,
While cookies bake, all turn to leer.
A little child, with eyes so bright,
Counts chocolate chips, a tasty bite.

The oven hums a silly tune,
As flour flies like animated dust, immune.
In aprons bright, they stomp around,
Making giggles the joyful sound.

Oh, how the marshmallows start to melt,
When roasted treats are gently dealt.
They bounce and giggle, fly off the stick,
'Cause fun and food feed laughter quick!

A dog sneaks in for crumbs to snatch,
With fluffy joys, he makes a match.
The sun pours in, a great delight,
As shadows dance with snacks tonight.

The Dance of Heat and Heart

In sweltering glow, the kids do play,
With lemonade stands on bright display.
They sell sweet dreams in cups of fun,
While racing leaps beneath the sun.

A silly hat atop each head,
It flops and jiggles, what a spread!
The splashes soar, a water fight,
With squeals and shouts that feel so right.

They bury toes in sandy bliss,
And make a mess, oh what a twist!
With ice cream cones, they run around,
Chasing giggles, joy unbound.

Each sunset brings a wiggly dance,
As shadows twirl in vibrant chance.
They cheer the warmth of laughter sweet,
In summer's glow, their hearts repeat.

A Symph of Light and Warmth

In the sky, it tosses gold,
Tickling clouds, it gets quite bold.
Squirrels gather for a dance,
While shadows prance in silly chance.

Lemons smile, they wear a grin,
As if they've had some lemon gin.
Flowers giggle, colors bright,
Chasing bugs in sheer delight.

Kissing the Horizon's Edge

A giant pancake up on high,
Winks at pies as they drift by.
It says to clouds, 'Come join my show!'
While birds dive in to steal the glow.

The grass feels warm, a comfy hug,
As ants parade, all snug as a bug.
They march like tiny soldiers proud,
While bees buzz by, they're quite loud!

Warm Embrace of Celestial Light

A playful ray does chase the ants,
While daisies tease, they do their dance.
Jellybeans rain from the blue,
While bunnies hop with nothing to rue.

Cotton candy clouds drift slow,
Pancakes flip, and syrup flows.
With laughter loud, the world's a feast,
As light and joy grow, never ceased.

Whispers of Light Through Trees

The trees tell jokes to passing leaves,
While squirrels giggle, pulling sleeves.
Bamboo bends, a bowing friend,
As feathered hats on branches blend.

Rays play peekaboo on barks,
While shadows dance like silly larks.
They poke and tease, and giggle clear,
Singing tunes for all to hear.

Glimmering Threads of Day

Morning breaks with a silly grin,
Coffee spills, let the chaos begin.
Light dances on my toast that I burn,
With each bite, it's my stomach I churn.

Birds chirp loudly, a raucous choir,
I join them, but they seem to retire.
Chasing shades, I think I'll take flight,
But tripping over my own feet is a plight.

Emotive Heat of a Gilded Sun

Under rays that tickle my skin,
A picnic starts with a cake and a grin.
Ants steal crumbs like little thieves,
While I chase them, feeling the breeze.

Ice cream melts faster than I can lick,
A sticky mess, oh, life is a trick!
Squirrels laugh, they hold their nuts tight,
While I'm left dreaming of a cool, sweet bite.

Kissed by Solar Symphony

Sunshine winks as I stroll outside,
My hat flies away, I just can't hide.
Caught in a laugh, my friends soon appear,
With sunglasses on, we look quite dear.

Chasing shadows, we think we're so cool,
Slipping on grass, oh, the day's a jewel!
The air's alive with giggles and shouts,
As the day unfolds, joy flutters about.

Radiance of Love's Awakening

Love blooms bright in this crazy sphere,
We share a laugh over pizza and beer.
Your smile shines like a beacon of light,
In my heart, you're a radiant sight.

Tickling toes in the warm summer glow,
We're dancing like dorks; let the world know!
Chasing the shadows, we let out a cheer,
For love in the sunshine brings joy to all here.

Light's Love on Nature's Canvas

A daisy wears shades, so chic and bright,
While crickets dance in the broad daylight.
Butterflies frolic, a colorful flight,
They're all fighting shadows—what a silly sight!

The trees don sun hats, quite snug on their bark,
Squirrels show off their acorns with a lark.
The flowers gossip, oh what a spark,
In this wild gallery where laughter leaves its mark!

Chasing the Solar Glow

A moth on a mission, so eager to meet,
Darts towards the lamp, thinking it's sweet.
"What's up with this light? It's no candy treat!"
He crashes, he flops, then he sheepishly retreats.

The shadows play tag in a quirky race,
A clumsy old turtle keeps losing the chase.
Fleas leap with flair, oh what a disgrace,
While ants march along, they can't keep their pace!

Sunlit Journeys Through Time

A clock on the wall, it giggles and twirls,
With hands that do tango and jump like girls.
"Time flies!" it declares, while the sunlight unfurls,
And the cat in the window gives lazy swirls.

The dog chases sunbeams, thinks they're a ball,
But they slip through his paws; oh, what a haul!
"Where are you, sunshine? I'm having a sprawl!"
That pup keeps on barking at shadows that crawl!

Embrace of Day's Radiance

The morning yawns wide, stretching out its rays,
Birds chirp a tune that's like cabaret plays.
With pancakes a-flying, oh what a craze,
As syrup cascades in sweet golden phase!

Then comes a butterfly, wearing a grin,
Sipping nectar while twirling, oh let's begin!
It's a party of petals, thick, soft, and thin,
In this frolic of quirks, let the fun times sin!

Glistening Bliss of Daylight

Golden rays tickle the trees,
Birds gossip as they tease.
A squirrel dances with slick moves,
While the cat just disapproves.

Daisies giggle in bright hues,
The grass whispers silly news.
As we slip on shades so bright,
Squinting at the joy of light.

Ice cream cones drip and melt,
Sticky fingers, happy yelps.
Laughter echoes through the park,
As we prance till it gets dark.

Flip-flops slap on the warm ground,
In sandals, joy is truly found.
Let's dance like nobody's here,
Until the stars begin to cheer.

Beacon of Hope

Roll out the picnic blanket wide,
A feast awaits, our joy, our pride.
Sandwiches stacked like mini towers,
Ants march in, demanding hours.

Kites soar high, with tails that flop,
A gentle breeze, we can't quite stop.
Soda cans pop with fizzy cheer,
As parents tell tales we've all heard here.

A rubber chicken squawks a tune,
Balloons dance and float to the moon.
With jokes aplenty and giggles galore,
Every moment makes our hearts soar.

Frolicking kids chase around,
While puppies bark with joy profound.
In this happy, sunlit sphere,
We find our laughter, loud and clear.

Sunbeam's Gentle Hold

Warm rays cuddle every cheek,
A glow so cheerful, never bleak.
Lazy hammocks sway in delight,
While the ice cream truck takes flight.

Chasing shadows, what a sight!
Friends playing tag until the night.
The grill sizzles with smoky smells,
While we share our wildest yells.

Jumping jacks and silly cheers,
With bright pink hats and goofy ears.
A cool drink spills; we laugh and share,
Who knew that laughter could fill the air?

As twilight whispers, "Play no more,"
We play hide and seek on the floor.
With sparkly lights above our heads,
We chuckle under our cozy beds.

Warmth Infused in Shadows

Squirrels play peek-a-boo, oh dear!
While cicadas serenade for cheer.
Shade beneath the leafy tree,
Where ridiculous faces roam free.

Slip-n-slide on a puddle's dare,
Squeals of laughter fill the air.
Wet socks squish, a silly plight,
Yet we smile through all the fright.

A paper boat floats with style,
Beauty in every childish smile.
Gather 'round for stories grand,
Where dragons dance and castles stand.

With every hug, and silly dance,
We sway together in a trance.
In shadows warm, we joke and play,
Forever locked in this bright day.

Saffron Tides of Laughter

The yellow glow brings joy to folks,
With every wink, the day just jokes.
Its cheeky rays tickle my nose,
A giggle here, a chuckle shows.

Balloons float high in the bright sphere,
While sandwiches dance without a care.
With a splash from the sparkling brook,
Nature's laughter, come take a look!

Birds sing tunes that just can't quit,
Charming squirrels doing their skit.
Sunbeams surf on the summer breeze,
Tickling everyone with such ease.

Even shadows join in the fun,
Tracing jokes as they run and run.
A festival where smiles collide,
In saffron tides, we laugh and glide.

Echoes of Day's Warmth

The light spills over hills so bright,
Sun-kissed muffins make taste buds bite.
A pancake flips, it lands on toes,
Breakfast giggles, how silly it goes.

With each ray, the bees start to hum,
They dance along, oh what a drum!
Around the park, kids scream with glee,
Chasing each other, just let it be!

The warm breeze whispers secret plays,
Tickling leaves in joyful ways.
As shadows play tag on the ground,
Pure laughter echoes all around.

So let's not waste this golden glow,
Join the parade, let laughter flow!
In the warmth of day's embrace,
We find pure joy in every space.

Sol's Gentle Lullaby

As the light strums across the lawn,
Flowers join in, bringing a yawn.
A breeze so soft that tickles your hair,
Spinning stories beyond compare.

The butterflies wear hats so fine,
"Do you see my colors shine?"
They flutter by with such a flair,
The garden giggles in warm air.

In this bliss, even dogs delight,
Chasing their tails, oh what a sight!
They tumble down in silly falls,
Whiskers twitching as nature calls.

So lay back and hear the tunes,
Of laughter sung by afternoon.
With every twirl, we join the sway,
In melodic fun of a sunlit day.

Serene Emotions in Glistening Rays

The glittering light skips on the pond,
Where frogs play chess and grow quite fond.
With winks and croaks, they rule the day,
Tadpoles laugh, "We're on our way!"

The trees wear smiles, their branches sway,
Dancing to echoes of soft ballet.
As squirrels prance, they play dress-up too,
In coats of sunshine, oh, what a view!

Each step we take on the warm ground,
Has comedy sprinkled all around.
From picnic ants to clouds that drift,
They share in joy, our hearts they lift.

So revel in rays that glisten bright,
Find the fun in pure daylight.
With serene emotions, let's embrace,
This quirky world, our joyful space.

Golden Caress of Daylight

When morning calls, I rise and grin,
The sun's a cheeky friend, let's begin!
It tickles my nose, makes me sneeze,
And whispers secrets through the trees.

The world's a stage, and I'm the star,
As rays of joy beam from afar.
I trip on shadows, laugh and roll,
With daylight's laughter, I feel whole.

Pancakes flip, and toast takes flight,
When sunlight dances, oh what a sight!
I slide on beams like a slippery eel,
That morning glow, oh what a deal!

So come, let's play in this golden cheer,
With all the quirks that we hold dear.
Each sunbeam's a prankster, shining bright,
In the fun-filled mornings, everything's right!

Radiant Morning Whisper

Awake! I hear a playful call,
That golden glow, it wants to brawl.
It tickles my toes, urges me out,
This silly dawn, it brings a shout!

Birds join in with their chirpy song,
As I bop my head, can't get it wrong.
Every ray is a jester's grin,
Turning simple moments into a win!

I race my shadow, can't catch a break,
It slyly sneaks while I'm on the lake.
A cup of joy spills, not a drop missed,
As morning laughs, I can't resist!

So let's wear these rays like a funny hat,
As we giggle and wiggle, imagine that!
The world is a circus, oh what a view,
In this radiant fun, let's paint it anew!

Dance of Dawn's Warmth

With each dawn, the world's a stage,
The warmth arrives with a cheeky page.
I twirl with shadows, laugh and sing,
As roosters join in, it's quite the fling!

Muffins bounce like they've got wings,
While toast competes in the morning flings.
Wobbly chairs join in, just for fun,
As I'm twirling 'round, oh how I run!

The rays poke fun with a playful tease,
Giving me a wink, making me freeze.
Yet here I stumble, giggles in the air,
In this dance of warmth, I haven't a care!

So grab a friend, let's jump and spin,
As morning's sunlight lets us in.
With silly moves and laughter galore,
Dawn's inviting song, forever we'll adore!

Light's Tender Horizon

When daylights come, all bets are off,
The horizon laughs, it's time to scoff.
I roll my eyes at clouds that play,
As colors burst in a wacky display!

Rainbows giggle, stretching wide,
While light bugs dart, taking pride.
A ticklish breeze gives hair a twirl,
In this funny light, I give a whirl!

I chase the giggles while they run,
With every step, more jokes begun.
Sunbeams dance like they're on a spree,
While shadows play a game of 'Catch Me!'

So let's embrace this whimsical tease,
With every ray, let's dance with ease.
In light's tender glow, we find our play,
Making memories that brightly stay!

A Tapestry of Light and Shadow

Dancing shadows in the park,
Waving to the chubby lark.
Sunbeams sneak under my hat,
Tickling me, oh isn't that fat?

A squirrel nods, wearing shades,
Grinning 'neath the leafy glades.
A cat sprawls, soaking in that cheer,
Dreaming of fish—what a career!

Clouds stroll by, don't take their time,
Making the sunlight tinged with rhyme.
They giggle, dance, and join the fray,
What a circus this bright day!

Let's toast to warmth and silly bliss,
With lemonade and a sun-kissed kiss.
So chase the rays, let laughter ring,
Life's a stage—go on, take wing!

Hues of Radiance Unfurled

Waking up with morning's grin,
The coffee pot is hissing—win!
Toast pops up in golden glee,
As if it knows it's meant for me.

Butter slides like a slippery fish,
It hops and jumps—a foodie wish!
The milk carton joins a dance,
Spilling over, quite by chance.

Birds in chorus sing out loud,
A feathered, furry, cheerful crowd.
They laugh at me—what a sight!
Who knew breakfast could take flight?

With a wiggle and a twirl,
I step into the world's bright whirl.
Sunshine laughs—oh what a tease,
It plays hide-and-seek with ease!

Morning's Gentle Glow

The curtains part, morning leaps,
A giggling breeze plays while it sweeps.
The breakfast table's set with joy,
A cereal box with a toy!

O Jell-O wiggles, what a sight!
Is that dessert for breakfast, right?
The toaster pops like fireworks,
Our laughter spreads like silly perks.

Doughnuts dance, all sugary and round,
They rolled off the plate, oh what a sound!
Chasing crumbs like little mice,
This morning's chaos is rather nice!

With smiles wide and spirits free,
We step out, joined in harmony.
Roaming the streets with playful glee,
What a wacky world, come dance with me!

Fields of Sunlit Dreams

Fields of gold stretch wide and bright,
A butterfly swings left and right.
It lands, takes a sip of nectar,
Playing tag, an eager specter.

Dandelions puff like little clouds,
I make wishes, shout them loud.
The wind chuckles, twirls my hair,
Carrying giggles everywhere.

Ladybugs in a dotty parade,
Marching round like they're well-made.
They wave their spots, so full of cheer,
As if to say, "Join the fun here!"

Let's tumble down the grassy hill,
With happy shouts, we all thrill.
Under the sky, bright and supreme,
We frolic in these sunlit dreams!

Embracing the Warmth Above

In the sky, a big ol' ball,
Warming all, from short to tall.
It tickles trees, it gives a cheer,
Like a bright clown with no fear.

Butterflies dance and bees just buzz,
While flowers grin, they know because.
A golden glow, a silly grin,
Makes everyone feel warm within.

The squirrels leap with giggly glee,
Even the rocks say, "Look at me!"
It's hard not to smile, run, and play,
When the bright orb has come to stay.

So grab some shades, let out a shout,
Spot the warmth you can't live without.
With each ray, there's joy in store,
Laughter echoes forevermore.

Daylight's Loving Hand

Morning breaks, it's time to rise,
With light pouring in, what a surprise!
The curtains dance, the shadows prance,
Life can't help but join the dance.

A fuzzy cat with sleepy eyes,
Paws at the light, oh, what a prize!
Chasing beams on the wooden floors,
Its happy purr sounds like applause.

Muffins baking, toast on high,
Even burnt, it's still a pie!
Daylight giggles, bright and bold,
Makes breakfast stories waiting to be told.

So here's to shenanigans galore,
With rays that knock upon your door.
Let's splash in puddles, shout hooray,
With daylight holding fun at bay!

Golden Touch of Dawn

As colors splash across the sky,
Birds chime in with a joyful cry.
A pancake flip, a syrup puddle,
The morning brings a wiggly cuddle.

Coffee brews like bubbling gold,
Chasing away the sleepy, cold.
A sunny wink from the floral bed,
Plants greet the day with a fun new spread.

The dog in shades, he strikes a pose,
While cats plot mischief, just like pros.
A warm embrace, a ticklish breeze,
Mischief whispers in the trees.

With hearts so light, we'll chase the beams,
Wrapped in laughter, spun from dreams.
Let's dance around as shadows fade,
In the warm light where pranks are made.

Warmth of a Radiant Soul

A glowing smile, a friendly face,
The warmth ignites the perfect space.
Like cookies fresh from the oven baked,
A joy-filled warmth that can't be faked.

Chasing umbrellas through gusty days,
We laugh at rain in amusing ways.
The puddles splash, a giggling race,
The warmth of joy is a bright embrace.

With sun-kissed cheeks, we skip along,
A silly dance to our own song.
Bright rays beckon us to explore,
Where laughter lives forevermore.

So gather 'round, let stories flow,
Under warmth that helps us grow.
With silly moments, hearts unfold,
In that bright glow, life turns to gold.

Glowing Tapestry of Emotions

In the morning, I squint tight,
Chasing shadows in the light.
My coffee spills, it starts to drip,
I laugh at my clumsy grip.

Birds dance on the window ledge,
In this life, I take a pledge.
To keep my hat on while I run,
And dance with glee, oh what fun!

Golden rays melt down the wall,
A light show, nature's playful ball.
I trip over my own two feet,
And bounce back up—what a treat!

With every giggle and each cheer,
The bright warmth banishes the fear.
Around we spin, no cares we keep,
In this glow, we laugh and leap!

Embrace of Gold and Blue

Golden rays tickle my nose,
While I try to strike a pose.
Waves crash with a playful sound,
In this joy, I'm turned around.

Splashing water on my shoes,
Unplanned dips? I'll gladly choose.
Sunshine laughs, it's quite the scene,
Imitating a tangerine.

With shades too bright, I cannot see,
I wink at clouds, they're winking me.
Tripping over sandy hills,
Who knew laughter could give chills?

Still, I choose to sway and spin,
With every gust, I dive right in.
The warm embrace, I won't let go,
Forever stuck in this bright flow!

Heartbeats in the Glow

Under the warmth, my heart skips beat,
Chasing shadows on tiny feet.
A friendly bug lands on my nose,
I giggle while my laughter flows.

Sun-kissed cheeks and funny faces,
I make silly moves in wild races.
A bird chirps in a cheeky tone,
Reminding me I'm not alone.

Tickled by warmth, I jump and sway,
A dance-off with my cat today.
We twirl and spin in this bright haze,
Creating laughs in silly ways.

And as the day begins to wane,
A gentle breeze blows away my pain.
With love and laughter intertwined,
In this glow, true joy we find!

Basking in Day's Illumination

Waking up with a silly grin,
Tiptoeing light, let the fun begin!
I put on shades, but they're upside down,
A sunny fool in a sunny town.

Today I'll bake some cookies bright,
But end up with a sticky fight!
The dough flies high, like rising suns,
My kitchen dance is full of puns.

Chasing clouds in the sky so blue,
I trip on grass, and out goes my shoe.
Laughter bubbles, it fills the air,
With every trip, I don't a care.

When evening falls, I wave goodbye,
To sunset colors in the sky.
In the golden glow, we'll reminisce,
A day well spent—a sunny bliss!

Echoes of Celestial Light

In the sky, a glowing sphere,
Dancing rays that bring us cheer.
But birds think it's a giant eye,
Winking down as they fly by.

With sunbeams tickling flowers' face,
They giggle in this warm embrace.
A butterfly in playful chase,
Stumbles on a leaf—what a race!

Clouds in jest play hide-and-seek,
While squirrels plot their sneaky peek.
'Is it dessert or just a tease?'
They ponder as they rustle leaves.

Laughter echoes in the light,
Nature's circus, what a sight!
With every shimmer, smiles grow broad,
Thank goodness for this sunny fraud!

Warmth in the Quiet Corners

In corners warm where shadows lie,
A cat is napping, dreams to fly.
With every beam that hits her nose,
She twitches paws as snores compose.

Dust motes dance like little sprites,
They're out to play, and oh, what sights!
A lazy dog joins in with flair,
Rolling 'round without a care.

The rooster crows, it sounds like fun,
A morning tune that's never done.
He struts about with head held high,
While chickens laugh and wonder why.

So in these nooks, where laughter's gold,
Life's simple joys continually unfold.
The warmth wraps us like a joke,
As we giggle 'neath this cozy cloak!

Radiance of Soothing Glow

A toaster pops with golden cheer,
Bread leaps high, it's breakfast here!
Cereal dances in the bowl,
As milk pours in to make it whole.

Jellybeans bask in radiant rays,
Holding candy parties for days.
They bounce around with silly glee,
Making sugar-fueled jubilee!

Outdoors, the grass starts telling tales,
Of silly ants on tiny trails.
"What's that critter with the hat?
A walking snack? Or just a brat?"

In golden light, we all conspire,
To share our dreams and rise higher.
With every giggle, life does flow,
In the glow, we steal the show!

Dawn's Embrace on Hidden Valleys

A valley wakes with yawns and stretches,
Bunnies hopping through soft wretches.
Sun rays paint the hills with zest,
As everyone prepares for jest.

The flowers bloom with silly hats,
And dance, oh dance, 'round lazy cats.
"Is it time for breakfast, friend?"
Their chirps and laughter never end.

Behind the hills, a sheep does prance,
Tripping on his comical stance.
He tumbled down with ruffled fleece,
Then boomed, "Who knew I'd be a beast?"

These hidden valleys hold such mirth,
In every corner, joy gives birth.
So let's enjoy this merry day,
In light and laughter, come what may!

Warm Emotions Under Sol's Gaze

Golden glow upon my face,
I dance like a silly ace.
With rays that tickle, laugh, and tease,
Nature's warmth, oh how it frees.

Sun hats worn, so broad and bright,
We bump and wander, pure delight.
A roast on grass, our picnic spreads,
While squirrels laugh at our misreads.

Bright balloons float in the air,
Chasing shadows, we haven't a care.
Twirl and twirl beneath the light,
In this warmth, every heart feels right.

With sunblock slathered from head to toe,
I'm part lobster, don't you know?
The heat's a friend, so full of cheer,
As we giggle, summer's here!

Eternal Glow of Affection

Radiant beams, they laugh and shine,
As we sip sodas, feel divine.
With every glimmer, laughter spreads,
Like radiant jelly on our breads.

A funny dance in the afternoon,
While bees buzz with a silly tune.
Kites above, now tangled tight,
We burst with laughter at this sight.

The heatwave offers quirky bliss,
As friends can't help but share a kiss.
But wait! Is that a bee on your nose?
We laugh so hard, who even knows?

With shades on, fashionably late,
Feeling cool while we impersonate.
The sun giggles down from above,
Wrapping us in its warmest love.

Promise in Every Ray

A golden glow upon my brow,
I promise I will eat this cow!
With shades of orange, pinks so bright,
We dine on food while feeling light.

Sipping ice tea, oh what a treat,
While ants march in their little beat.
They plot and plan their picnic raid,
While we munch on fries, unafraid.

Every ray a funny chance,
For awkward moves and crazy dance.
With SPF fifty to the max,
I'm shielded from those burning tracks.

In the warmth, we gather cheer,
Confetti laughs, like summer's beer.
As shadows grow long and dreams awake,
Our hearts as light as cake and flake.

Chasing Beams of Affection

I'm chasing rays like radar blips,
Dodging sunburns and summer trips.
With pals who giggle in their hats,
We run like confused, buzzing gnats.

A frisbee soars, my aim is wild,
It lands on someone's sunburnt child!
Sorry dude, but laugh we must,
In rays of warmth, we find our trust.

Lemonade spills, and what's that splash?
Wet clothes bring a funny bash.
Water fights with squeezy toys,
In the sun, we are just pure joys.

Chasing down beams with silly glee,
Under a bright cherry tree.
With each giggle, the memories stay,
Embodied in warmth, come what may!

Softer Shades of Solar Love

Golden rays make us feel so fine,
Spilled on breakfast, oh what a sign!
Butter on toast, a sunny delight,
Even the coffee is dancing in light.

Bouncing off roofs, a playful glare,
Chasing the shadows, without a care!
Cats in the window are soaking it in,
Dreaming of mice, with a cheeky grin.

Pigeons are strutting, feeling quite bold,
Strutting like models in outfits of gold.
Even the flowers are swaying to tune,
Giggling softly, beneath the soft moon.

So grab a sandwich, let laughter ignite,
Under the glow, everything feels right.
The day is a jest, let's celebrate play,
In this golden glow, we frolic and sway.

Glow of Endless Hope

A hat on my head, it's a bright sunny day,
Too much sunscreen? Oh well, hooray!
Icicles melting, they were quite a sight,
Now they're just puddles, with no chance to bite.

The garden is buzzing with bees on a spree,
Sipping on nectar, all happy and free.
Dandelions giggle, proud of their fluff,
They don't mind the wind, they're tough enough!

With lemonade glasses that clink in delight,
We'll toast to the shadows that dance in the light.
A world full of laughter, why take it so grim?
Join in the jest, let's all sing on a whim!

As clouds play tag with a mischievous glow,
We skip all around, in a whimsical flow.
So here's to the bright, and the laughter we share,
Under the glow, life's a carnival fair!

Light's Harmonious Embrace

Twinkle, twinkle, little rays,
Flowers making funny bouquets!
The grass looks greener, oh what a show,
Even worms are dancing, just look at them go!

Ice cream mishaps, a cone on the floor,
Laughter erupts as we run for more.
Kites in the sky, with tricks up their sleeves,
Tangled up strings, that's what summer leaves!

Bananas and flip-flops, quite the strange mix,
Why do we trip? It's all in the tricks!
Sunbathing dogs with their floppy ears,
Rolling around, forgetting their fears.

Meet me at noon, where the shadows are small,
Celebrating warmth with a bright summer ball.
With giggles and glances, let's dance all night,
In this harmony, everything feels right!

Mosaic of Light and Warmth

Checkered blankets on the green grass terrain,
Spilling some juice, oh what a stain!
Picnics transform into a laugh-out-loud,
Sandwiches flying, oh aren't we so proud?

The cat's in the shade, avoiding the heat,
Plotting a scheme on how to be fleet.
Chasing its tail in a circular flight,
Wondering who put up this quirky light!

With sun hats galore, we gather around,
Chasing our shadows, they hardly can't be found.
Tickling toes in the warm summer breeze,
Wishing for naps, but who's got the keys?

So toast to the warmth, with a splash of delight,
In this colorful chaos, everything's right.
With humor and joy, let the light flood our days,
In this crazy dance, we cheerfully blaze!

Brightened Paths of Serenity

In morning light, the coffee brews,
My slippers squeak, I trip on shoes.
The cat's on the table, quite a sight,
As I chase the toast, oh what a plight!

Laughter spills with each little mishap,
My jam's a mess, like a sticky trap.
But with each giggle and playful cheer,
The day starts bright, let's make it clear!

Dancing shadows on walls so bold,
The warmth wraps 'round, a hug to hold.
With silly socks and mismatched flair,
Who knew a morning could be so rare?

So let the light guide our foolish ways,
Through quirky moments that fill our days.
With each stumble, we find our stride,
In this joyful journey, we won't hide!

Golden Threads of Connected Dreams

In playful beams, the squirrels prance,
A game of tag, a wild dance.
They chatter loudly, wings in flight,
As I wave back, what a funny sight!

The breeze decides to mess my hair,
With leaves a-twirling everywhere.
A snapshot taken, all aglow,
We laugh so hard; where did time go?

Bright petals fall, like confetti here,
A wobbly dance, with cheer and cheer.
Who knew that laughter could unite,
In dandelion fields, such sheer delight?

With each shared joke, a bond we weave,
As sunlight plays, we dare to believe.
Connected dreams in this golden brew,
Happy memories formed, just us two!

Sunswept Heartstrings

With rays that tickle, skies so blue,
I'm chasing shadows, joining the crew.
The ice cream melts; it's dripping fast,
A race against time, make this summer last!

A giggle here, a skip right there,
My friend does a dance without a care.
With sprinkles flying, laughter's the key,
In this sunswept world, we're wild and free!

The hammock sways, we swing and swing,
With silly faces, we wear the bling.
In golden hours, a chorus sings,
As lighthearted joy is the song that clings!

So gather your pals, let's steal the scene,
In a field of sunshine, life's a dream.
With every heartbeat, our fun expands,
In this whimsical land, we make our plans!

Hallowed by Dappled Light

Amid the trees, where sunlight weaves,
The picnic spread has got us in thieves.
A sandwich flies, oh what a throw,
As laughter echoes, we steal the show!

With dappled light doing its trick,
We're dodging ants that scamper quick.
Everyone's munching, way too much bread,
The jello wobbles, all colors spread!

A hat goes flying, the breeze takes hold,
We chase it down as the stories unfold.
With silly hats and mismatched fun,
In this quirky tale, we've truly won!

So let's embrace this playful scene,
With each new giggle, our hearts convene.
Hallowed by humor, we'll dance till night,
In laughter and joy, our spirits ignite!

Solstice of Comfort

On a summer's day, my ice cream melts,
As I chase the sun, it laughs and pelts.
Those squirrels in shades wear tiny hats,
They dance in circles like playful cats.

With lemonade in hand, I sip and grin,
As rays of sunshine tickle my chin.
The grill is hot, the burgers sing,
While neighbors join in, that summer fling.

Flip-flops flapping, my toes in sand,
Big hats collide, it's all unplanned.
We nap in hammocks, swaying slow,
While ants steal our snacks, oh, what a show!

With skies so bright, we chase fireflies,
Oranges and yellows light up our sighs.
In this sun-soaked chaos, laughs abound,
In every corner, joy can be found.

Twilight's Silent Warmth

At dusk, the bugs throw a little rave,
Moths in disco lights, the light we crave.
A chilly breeze steals my warm delight,
The lawn chairs wobble, oh what a sight!

Cicadas chirp their evening tune,
While we share stories beneath the moon.
A glow on the grill, it's time to feast,\nWho knew roasting marshmallows would be the least?

Why do the stars twinkle, I wonder aloud,
As a raccoon peeks, feeling quite proud.
The night wears shades of orange and pink,
As neighbors shout, "Pass that drink!"

Fireflies dance and wiggle around,
I swear they're trying to be profound.
In twilight's hug, all worries fade,
While laughter lingers like a sweet cascade.

Dawn's Tender Glow

Morning rays peek through the blinds,
Coffee brews, stirring sleepy minds.
A rooster crows with a sassy flair,
Pajamas waving like they don't care.

Cats stretch wide as if they own the space,
While I stumble in a sleepy race.
Toast pops up, a golden surprise,
Funny faces toast, what a prize!

Birds chirp songs, with giggles to share,
They may not dance, but oh do they dare!
Joggers zoom past in fluorescent shoes,
Chasing their health while I snooze the news.

In this sunrise, laughter ignites,
Chasing away the sleepy fights.
With breakfast mess, and spills galore,
Every dawn beckons us for more!

Illuminating Heartbeats

With sunlight streaming through my door,
Socks mismatched, oh what a score!
Dance parties start with no real plan,
Bumping and grinding, a silly clan.

Radiant beams bring the giggles out,
As I trip on my dog, oh what a clout!
Chasing shadows, we play hide and seek,
My friends shout, "Sunshine, you're such a freak!"

Picnics sprawled on a checkered sheet,
With ants on the side, they join our feat.
Silly stories of our childhood days,
In golden light, we laugh and praise.

With twilight's glow, we wrap it tight,
The warmth of joy, it feels so right.
In every heartbeat, sunshine finds,
A playful dance that intertwines.

Emblazoned Skies at Dusk

The sky wore a grin, so bright and bold,
Colors danced around, like stories told.
Chasing shadows with a playful glee,
Even the clouds were laughing, you see!

A flamingo tried to take to the air,
But tripped on its wings, oh what a scare!
The stars whispered secrets in a soft lilt,
While rabbits hee-hawed, dressed in bright quilt.

Fireflies twinkled like mischievous sprites,
Writing their names in the summer nights.
With a wink and a nod, they'd swirl and sway,
For this was a time to frolic and play!

As the evening wore on, they gathered round,
Frogs sang their songs in a humorous sound.
The moon had a chuckle, said, "Join the fun!"
And painted the world till the night was done!

Sweetness of Golden Hours

In the kitchen, chaos whirled like a breeze,
With cookies on shelves and crumbs with great ease.
Mom's apron was smeared with sprinkles and dough,
The cake on the counter was a formidable foe!

Baking soda sprinkled like magic dust,
As flour went flying, oh, what a must!
Giggles erupted as cupcakes took flight,
Frosting looked like a monster—what a sight!

The candy jar jived like it owned the room,
While gummy bears plotted their sweet little doom.
Pies rolled their eyes as we tasted each treat,
"Not everyone loves us, but we can't be beat!"

So we danced in the kitchen without a care,
Mixing and munching, what fun to share!
In the sweetness of hours, our laughter would flow,
For every bite tasted would steal the show!

Halo of Morning's Promise

Mornings come in with a splash of cheer,
Roosters crow loudly, insisting they're here.
Coffee spills over, what a sight to see,
The dog thinks it's breakfast, but it's just for me!

Toast pops up like it's jumping for fame,
While jam's on the counter, playing the game.
The cat's on the table, ready to pounce,
On a plate of pancakes, it's quite the trounce!

Birds sing their songs, but they can't hit the note,
It sounds like a symphony stuck in a boat.
Butterflies flutter with a whimsical laugh,
Whispering secrets to the sun's golden half.

With each crack of dawn, a circus takes flight,
In the lively chaos, the world feels just right.
Morning's promise is sealed with a grin,
As we dive into breakfast and let the day begin!

Sanctuary of Hearth and Light

Home is a roast, that's a fact we agree,
With laughter and warmth, it's where we all flee.
The couch claims its throne with cushions galore,
While popcorn's been scattered, oh, what a chore!

The cat takes a leap, chasing shadows anew,
Trips over the rug—just one and then two!
Family tales spun like wild little threads,
As the dog sticks his nose where the mischief spreads.

The fireplace crackles, swapping stories untold,
As blankets wrap 'round us, keeping us bold.
Sweaters are worn like a big fuzzy hug,
While snacks sit upon our knees, snug as a bug.

In this sanctuary, giggles abound,
With each turn of a joke, joy is found.
As the night gathers close, we bask in delight,
In our cozy little world, everything's right!

Light Weaver's Serenade

In the morning light, so bright and clear,
A cat does dance, without any fear.
He pounces at shadows, a silly old sport,
Thinking he's fierce, but he's just short.

The coffee brews up, it starts to steam,
As I find my sock, what a silly theme.
Chasing the rays, I twirl and I spin,
Pretending I'm graceful but trip on my chin.

In the park, I see dogs take flight,
Chasing their tails, in pure delight.
Round and round, they run with glee,
I laugh so hard, they look just like me!

As I bask in this brilliant glow,
I wonder if plants think humans are slow.
For as we admire, they grow and spread,
While we trip over roots, trying not to dread!

Caress of Daybreak's Glow

The rooster crows loud, what a funny sound,
As I stumble about, my socks not around.
A squirrel's in my yard, with a nut it clings,
Doing acrobatics, it's got such spring!

Pancakes flip high, oh what a mess!
Syrup takes flight, I must confess.
Fluffy clouds float 'cross the bright blue sky,
While I argue with toast, No! It's not dry!

A toddler nearby giggles at a bee,
Swatting the air, feeling so free.
She proclaims, "It's a dog, not a bug!"
I nod and agree; I'm giving her a hug!

As day moves along, with laughter and cheer,
I chase after dreams, refusing to fear.
Let's laugh at the silliness, embrace it all,
In this bright golden glow, we stand tall!

Sunlit Whispers

In the yard, a flower starts to bloom,
Whispering secrets, making clouds fume.
A bumblebee buzzes, it thinks it's so cool,
While tripping on petals, oh what a fool!

Children with kites run, screeching with glee,
Flying high up, as happy as could be.
But just one small gust brings chaos and fright,
Kites tangled up, what a comical sight!

Birds chirp sweet songs, thinking they're stars,
While a dog beside me gleans out of cars.
"Hey look at me, I'm the king of the park!"
Yet all he has done is leave quite the mark!

Laughter erupts, as shadows dance wide,
In the warmth of the glow, all cares we hide.
With joy in our hearts, we take in the show,
In this dazzling light, let's all let it flow!

Embrace of Horizon's Fire

A frog jumps high on a lily pad,
With a great big splash, it makes me glad.
It croaks out a tune, thinking it's a star,
While the dragonflies buzz and fly near and far.

Picnics spread out with treats all around,
Sandwiches tumble, they're hardly profound.
Chips crunch and scatter, it's quite a mess,
But giggling mischief brings nothing but bliss!

A bear in my garden thinks he owns the place,
Chasing me off with a curious face.
As I wave him goodbye, with a laugh and a grin,
He snickers back, in his furry old skin!

Through giggles and mess, we soak in the cheer,
In this bright wonderland, no room for fear.
We dance with delight till the sky turns to night,
In this wacky warm glow, everything feels right!

Nurtured by Solar Flare

I danced with shadows, oh what a delight,
The cat chased beams, a comical sight.
Birds in sunglasses, singing away,
I laughed so hard, I brightened the day.

Sipping on nectar, bees buzzing around,
They think they're stylish, with pollen they're crowned.
A sunburnt squirrel looks quite absurd,
Wearing a hat made of peanut and fur.

Daydreaming of warmth, I hear laughter loud,
The flowers are giggling, they draw quite a crowd.
With petals like skirts, they twirl in a breeze,
"Come join the party!" they joyfully tease.

Even the grass wears a golden hue,
Tickling my toes, oh, who knew it knew?
Blinded by rays, I stumble and sway,
Tripping on sunlight, come laugh with me, hey!

Enchanted by the Gilded Sky

A sunbeam rode in on a jellybean cloud,
Whispering secrets, it feels oh so proud.
An umbrella's up when it's sunny and clear,
But it's just for the juice of my midday beer.

Chasing the shadows, oh what a chase,
A raccoon in shades, oh look at that face!
He's stealing my snacks without even a care,
We giggle together, what a funny affair.

The daisies are winking with cheeky delight,
While I tell my jokes, their petals take flight.
A snail in a turtleneck, what a surprise,
He's slow on the punchline but wise in his guise.

With giggles and grins, the world seems so bright,
Under the laughter that dances in light.
So come join the fun, don't be caught in a rut,
Let's embrace the shenanigans, no ifs, ands, or but!

When Light Meets Heart

The clumsy old lamp just spills out its cheer,
Flickering bright, as if saying, "I'm here!"
Crickets sing ballads, creating a scene,
While frogs in tuxedos hop like a dream.

Picnics on rooftops, with snacks piled so high,
The ants throw a party, they've all come to spy.
"Who invited the crumbs?" they grumble with zeal,
While dancing and prancing, they pirouette real.

A butterfly's hat made of leaf and of flair,
Twirling through daisies, without a care.
A dog in a bowtie joins in with a bark,
He winks and he nods as he chases the spark.

With a twinkle and giggle, they all gather 'round,
In this luminous chaos, our laughter is found.
As light meets the heart, oh what a sweet fate,
We're all in this dance — so come on, don't wait!

Emotions Wrapped in Light

In a world made of giggles wrapped soft in the glow,
A hedgehog with glasses steals popcorn to show.
He munches and crunches, a sight to behold,
Sharing a wink as the stories unfold.

Wrapped in bright ribbons, the sunflowers sway,
"Join our parade!" they merrily say.
With stems like confetti, they wiggle and prance,
Trying to pull me into their dance.

A lizard in overalls plays the guitar,
Crooning for joy, my star of the hour.
While shadows sway gently, they clap in delight,
With laughter and joy, we all share the night.

As emotions unfold like the petals in bloom,
I chuckle at moments brightening the room.
Come join the laughter, it's a party of glee,
In this radiant world, we're all truly free!

Sunlit Dreams in Shimmering Waves

Waves splash and giggle, a sea of delight,
Seagulls wearing hats take off in flight.
Crabs play the conga, oh what a scene,
Beach balls are bouncing, if you know what I mean!

Sandy toes wiggle, the sun starts to grin,
Even the fishes decide to join in.
Flip-flops are dancing on the shoreline's tune,
While dolphins do backflips under the moon!

Kites in the sky are having a race,
While jellyfish dance in their jelly-like grace.
Oh, what a party, every wave brings a cheer,
Where laughter and sunlight are always near!

So grab your sunscreen, join the fun spree,
In this wavy world, you're wild and so free.
With dreams in the sunlight, come take a dive,
In shimmering waves where the giggles thrive!

Celestial Embrace of Day

A golden pancake sizzles in the sky,
Toast pops up, saying, "Oh my, oh my!"
The coffee pot's bubbling, a dance at the brew,
While shadows pirouette, as morning shines through.

Cats stretch like taffy, yawning with grace,
Chasing sunbeams, leaving a furry trace.
Birds in their tuxedos sing tunes to impress,
While squirrels negotiate over acorns, no less!

The mailman's got jokes, as he delivers the mail,
With the sun warming up on his balmy trail.
Kids in their shorts are treating grass like a dance,
Throwing boomerangs, hoping to take a chance!

So raise up your toast to the day that unfurls,
With laughter and light, let the fun give you twirls.
In this radiant realm, where silly rules sway,
Let's charm the bright hours, come laugh and just play!

Dance Upon the Light

Twinkle toes tap on warm golden rays,
The sidewalk's a stage for hilarious plays.
With shadows as partners, we strut and we sway,
While giggles escape in a playful ballet!

Butterflies waltz on a zephyr's embrace,
Taking care not to ruin their lovely lace.
Kids in a circle spin wildly around,
While hummingbirds hover, in laughs they're unbound.

Puppies go skittering, barking in glee,
Chasing the light as if it were free.
Laughter erupts from the trees high above,
Where squirrels play tag, filled with joy and love.

So join in the frolic, let your worries take flight,
In this dazzling dance where we bask in the light.
With every bright moment and smile that takes flight,
Let's cherish the joy that we find in the light!

Horizons Painted in Gold

Crayons are melting across the blue sky,
As colors collide, they giggle and fly.
A rainbow of laughter drips down from above,
While clouds play hopscotch in a dance full of love.

Turtles in glasses enjoy sunburst delight,
While ants throw a party that lasts through the night.
Kites are creating a gallery up high,
With a canvas of smiles, we let worries fly.

The wind whispers secrets, tickling the trees,
While flowers compete for the biggest bee tease.
Painted horizons with hues made so bold,
Capture the joy in these moments of gold!

So giggle together, and marvel at this,
For laughter and colors bring moments of bliss.
In this vibrant spectacle, remember it's true,
Life's funniest moments are painted for you!

Emblazoned Echoes of Love

A bright balloon floats high above,
Chasing shadows, like a silly dove.
With laughter loud and cheers sincere,
We dance like clowns, our joy is clear.

In puddles splashed, we make our mark,
Stomp our feet, our song a lark.
Kites weave tales in swirling air,
While whispers of ice cream fill the square.

Waffle cones and sprinkles bright,
Chasing friends into the night.
Bumbling 'round with goofy grins,
In this parade, everyone wins!

So grab a friend and join the play,
In silly hats, we seize the day.
For in this moment, small and grand,
We echo love across the land.

Glimmer in the Evening's Light

Twinkling stars and moths that dance,
A firefly joins, it takes a chance.
We giggle loud as shadows blend,
In nighttime's glow, let laughter mend.

We twirl around with socks askew,
Like drunken ducks in shades of blue.
The moon's a grin, its beams a tease,
While whispers tickle through the trees.

With friends in tow, we sing with pride,
In glittering moments, we shall glide.
A game of tag beneath the sky,
Chasing moonbeams, oh so spry!

So raise a toast to silly nights,
With cups held high, let's share our sights.
For in this hour, glee takes flight,
With merry hearts, we claim the night.

Shimmering Pathways to Bliss

A candy trail leads big and small,
With jellybeans and cakes to brawl.
On sugar clouds, we bounce and roll,
In this sweet land, we find our soul.

Lollipops whisper secret tunes,
While gummy bears become our goons.
As chocolate rivers flow with glee,
We'll feast like kings, just you and me.

Jumping high on marshmallow dreams,
With silly hats and goofy schemes.
We garden flowers made of pies,
In this delight, the spirit flies.

So take a taste of joyful cheer,
In this realm, we hold so dear.
Hand in hand, let's dash and spin,
On shimmering pathways, let fun begin!

Illuminated Moments of Joy

A party hat on every head,
With cupcakes piled, they all want bread.
Balloons take flight like silly dreams,
While laughter bursts at all the seams.

Confetti falls like candy rain,
As clowns juggle, without a strain.
Sock puppets dance in wild delight,
In moments where the world feels right.

We'll paint our faces, giggles grow,
As silly antics steal the show.
With friends beside, let spirits soar,
In this bright joy, who could ask for more?

So take a leap, don't hesitate,
As we create, let's celebrate!
These moments, they are ours to keep,
In the glow of joy, a blissful leap.

Dance of Sol's Splendor

When daylight breaks with a grin,
The roosters crow, let the fun begin.
Shadows stretch like they're in a race,
Chasing the light, oh, what a trace!

The sun wears shades, looking so cool,
Warming the world, like a golden pool.
Flowers giggle as they open wide,
In this bright party, they take pride.

Clouds show up, trying to be the star,
But they just float, not getting far.
Sunbeams twirl, it's their daily jig,
Bouncing off rooftops, oh, so big!

At noon, it's a sizzling affair,
Bees buzzing loudly, flying with flair.
Grab your lemonade, let's raise a glass,
To the golden orb that makes us laugh!

Luminous Hues of Morning

Morning peeks with a cheeky laugh,
Painting the world with a joyful half.
Birds serenade from trees so high,
As the hues dance, it's a vibrant sky.

Coffee spills like a work of art,
Steam curling, warming every heart.
Socks mismatched, oh, what a sight,
As we embrace this quirky light.

The kitchen's a stage for toast to fly,
Jam splattered, oh my, oh my!
Butter slides down, what a great mess,
But in this chaos, we feel blessed.

With laughter echoing, we twirl and spin,
Bathing in warmth, let the day begin.
Each moment shines like a brilliant bow,
In playful colors, our mood will glow!

Radiant Light's Affection

Daybreak whispers, 'Rise, don't be late,'
As we wiggle from sleep, it's truly great.
Pajamas on, it's a colorful sight,
With sunshine giggling, what pure delight!

Breakfast dances with sunny flair,
Pancakes flipping, syrup in the air.
Fruits and cereal join in the fun,
Together they cheer, 'We're number one!'

Outside, squirrels are having a race,
Chasing shadows, all over the place.
The grass tickles toes, as we prance,
In this golden glow, we find our dance.

So let's gather 'round, and share the joy,
With silly hats, and a new toy.
Laughter wrapped in warm embrace,
In this radiant light, we find our place!

Kiss of Day's Radiance

When the day wakes with a sunny kiss,
Everything smiles—it's a moment of bliss.
Cats stretch out like they own the street,
Chasing the sunlight, they dance on their feet.

Picnics loaded with sandwiches stacked,
Ants march in lines, oh, how they act!
Waves of laughter on this bright track,
As we spill our drinks, there's no turning back.

Sun hats on, divided by style,
Wide-brimmed, floppy, making us smile.
Sunscreen lathered like frosting on cake,
In this radiant glow, we'll never shake.

As evening tips its hat to the day,
Fireflies burst out, lighting our play.
Let's dance with shadows, twirl till we tire,
In this radiant spectacle, we feel inspired!

www.ingramcontent.com/pod-product-compliance
Lightning Source LLC
Chambersburg PA
CBHW072216070526
44585CB00015B/1362